The Ultimate Guide with 111 Top Tips on Saving Money

The Ultimate Guide with 111 Top Tips on Saving Money

Proven and Unexpected Real-Life Strategies for Families to Cut Costs, Build Resilience, and Thrive in Any Economy

Home Sweet Home Publishing

Copyright 2025, Home Sweet Home Publishing (Aria Capri International Inc). All rights reserved.

Authors:
Home Sweet Home Publishing
Mauricio Vasquez

First Printing: April 2025

ISBN 978-1-998729-34-0 (Electronic book)
ISBN 978-1-998729-33-3 (Hardcover book)
ISBN 978-1-998729-32-6 (Paperback)

Disclaimer

The information provided in this book is for educational and informational purposes only. It is designed to offer general money-saving ideas and personal finance strategies for families and individuals seeking to manage household expenses better and make thoughtful financial choices.

This book is not a substitute for personalized financial, legal, tax, insurance, investment, accounting, or other professional advice. While the strategies, examples, and tools included may reflect real-life situations and aim to empower readers to make smarter decisions, every family's financial situation is unique. Readers are strongly encouraged to seek guidance from qualified professionals familiar with their specific needs and circumstances before implementing any financial, legal, or tax-related decisions.

The author and publisher have made reasonable efforts to ensure the accuracy and completeness of the information contained herein at the time of publication. However, laws, regulations, markets, and personal finance best practices may change over time, and the applicability of specific tips may vary depending on geographic location or evolving family needs.

No guarantees are made regarding the results you may achieve. Savings and financial progress will vary based on individual income levels, lifestyle habits, market conditions, and personal effort. The author does not assume liability for any loss or damages, financial or otherwise, resulting from the use of this material.

By reading this book, you agree that the author and publisher are not responsible for your financial decisions nor for any positive or negative outcomes that may result from implementing the presented ideas or recommendations.

Always use your judgment, research, and consult trusted professionals when managing your financial future.

Dear Reader,

As a fellow parent and the author of this guide, I appreciate your feedback.

It only takes a moment—just scan the QR code to leave a quick review.

Your review helps more families discover this book, take control of their finances, and build greater resilience and peace of mind.

Thank you for being part of this mission to help families thrive—one wise money choice at a time.

All the best,

Mauricio

Want 111 More Smart Money-Saving Tips?

You've already taken a decisive step by purchasing this guide. Now let me send you 111 more practical, proven, and creative tips—designed to help your family cut costs, reduce stress, and thrive in any economy.

✔ These bonus tips are NOT in the book
✔ They're yours FREE as a thank-you for being a reader
✔ Delivered straight to your inbox—so you can keep saving, week after week

To access your 111 additional money-saving tips, scan this QR code:

Join thousands of families building financial peace—one wise decision at a time.

We're in this together. Let's keep going.

Mauricio

Do You Need a Little Extra Support to Stay on Track?

We've created the Money-Smart Family Toolkit to help you take what you will learn in this book even further. This collection of practical, printable planners and trackers is designed to help you **stay organized, reduce stress, and build real financial momentum** starting today.

These downloadable tools are perfect for busy families who want to stay organized, make steady progress, and turn smart money habits into everyday wins.

Trackers available include:
1. Assignment Tracker Sheet Planner
2. Debt Snowball Tracker
3. Expense Tracker Planner
4. Food Weekly Meal Planner
5. Goal Tracker Sheet Planner
6. Income Tracker Planner
7. Monthly Budget Planner
8. Mood Tracker Planner
9. Savings Challenge Planner

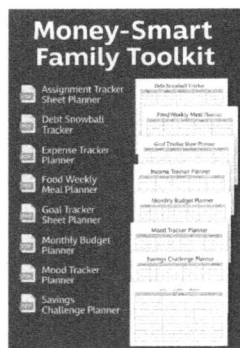

Scan the QR code to explore the complete set and see how these tools can support your journey.

Make your goals visual. Make your progress visible.

INTRODUCTION

Let's be honest: managing money isn't just about numbers—it's about trade-offs. It's about stretching every dollar while giving yourself and your family a joyful life. It's about navigating rising costs, uncertain economies, and endless responsibilities, all while wondering, *"Are we doing enough?"*

If that sounds familiar, you're not alone—and in the right place.

This book was written for families like yours—hardworking, thoughtful, and doing their best to make smart financial decisions without sacrificing what matters most. Maybe you're looking for ways to save on groceries, lower your utility bills, or finally get a handle on budgeting. Perhaps you're trying to prepare for the future while living fully today. This guide will meet you wherever you are on your journey—with real-life, practical strategies that work.

Why This Book Is Different

Unlike many finance books with theory, jargon, or one-size-fits-all solutions, this guide is built around actionable tips across 24 key household expense categories. These are the same categories families spend on every single day—like groceries, housing, transportation, utilities, childcare, health, and even mindset and habits.

Each tip is designed to help you:

- Cut costs without cutting joy.

- Stretch your income without working more hours.

- Build resilience so you're better prepared for whatever comes next.

You won't find complicated spreadsheets or generic advice here. Instead, you'll get **clear, encouraging, step-by-step ideas** that fit your busy life.

Small Changes Add Up

The truth is, you don't need to overhaul your entire lifestyle to make a meaningful difference. Often, the small, consistent changes—the five-minute adjustments, the second thoughts before clicking "buy now," the intentional meal plans—help you keep more of your hard-earned money.

By applying just a few of these tips, you may immediately start seeing extra savings. Over time, those savings grow, your stress goes down, and your confidence goes up.

Even better? Many of the tips in this book don't just save money—they build good habits, strengthen your family routine, and create space for the things that matter: connection, health, security, and peace of mind.

You Deserve Financial Peace—Without Perfection

This isn't about being perfect. It's about being *intentional.* Every family's situation is different, and every tip in this book is meant to be flexible. Take what fits. Adapt what needs tweaking. Leave what doesn't serve you. The goal isn't to restrict your life—it's to empower you to live it on your terms, with more freedom and less financial pressure.

Let's Begin—One Tip at a Time

As you move through these pages, you'll discover everything from budgeting hacks and shopping strategies to mindset shifts and printable tools that support real progress. This book is designed to be your go-to reference—something you can return to repeatedly, no matter the season or stage of life.

So take a deep breath, grab a pen, and let's get started. You don't need to do everything. You just need to do something—today.

HOW TO USE THIS BOOK

There's no one-size-fits-all path to saving money—because no two families live the same life.

This book was designed to be flexible, practical, and ready for the real world. Whether you're just starting your financial journey or looking for fresh ideas to level up your savings game, you'll find strategies here that meet you where you are.

Here are a few ways readers like you may find the most value:

Many readers begin by flipping through the 23 household spending categories and jumping straight to the areas most matter to them. If groceries are eating up your income, start there. If your utility bills spike every winter, head to that section first. This book is built so you can go directly to what's relevant without reading it front to back.

Others prefer to read the book cover to cover, taking notes or highlighting as they go. This gives a full-picture view of where your money's going—and where hidden opportunities might be hiding.

Focusing on one tip a day for the next 30 days is also helpful. This makes change manageable and builds confidence with small, steady wins. If you enjoy structure and habit-building, this method works wonders.

This book can also spark fun and meaningful conversations for families with kids. You could turn it into a weekly family money challenge—pick one new tip each week, try it together, and celebrate your success at the end of the week. You're not just saving—you're teaching values and building shared habits that last.

And, of course, this book is designed to be a trusted reference whenever life throws something new your way. Whether you're moving, changing jobs, preparing for a baby, or dealing with rising costs, you can come back to these pages for clarity, support, and simple ideas that work.

TABLE OF CONTENTS

1. GROCERIES & MEAL PLANNING

1. Shop Your Pantry Before Buying More

Summary:
Before heading to the grocery store, take stock of what's already in your pantry, fridge, and freezer. It helps you avoid buying duplicates and saves money.

Why This Works:
Most families have forgotten cans of soup, half-full pasta boxes, or produce nearing expiration. By using what you already have, you stretch your budget further and reduce unnecessary food waste. Studies show the average family wastes $1,300 in food annually. That's real money lost in spoiled or overlooked items. Shopping your pantry first trims your grocery bill, forcing more mindful meal planning and smarter shopping habits.

How to Do It:

- Set a 10-minute "pantry check" before planning meals.

- Jot down what needs to be used first.

- Search for recipes using those items.

- Plan meals that fill the gaps, not repeat what you already own.

- Shop only for true missing ingredients.

---

2. Cook Once, Eat Twice

Summary:
Make more significant portions during dinner, use leftovers for lunch, or transform them into a new meal the next day. This reduces prep time and food costs.

Why This Works:
Instead of cooking from scratch every night or buying lunch out, repurposing leftovers lowers food waste and saves on groceries. For example, a $12 homemade chilli can feed four people twice—cutting your cost per meal in half. It's also perfect for busy weeknights or when you're tempted to order takeout. Cooking once and eating twice saves time, money, and stress.

How to Do It:

- Double recipes for dinners that reheat well (soups, casseroles, pasta).

- Use leftovers creatively—chicken becomes wraps, veggies become stir-fry.

- Pack lunch portions right after dinner.

- Label and freeze extra food to avoid boredom.

- Keep a "leftover night" night a week to clean out the fridge.

---

3. Switch to Store Brands

Summary:
Choose store-brand versions of everyday groceries like

cereal, pasta, and canned goods. They're often just as good and significantly cheaper.

Why This Works:
Store-brand items are typically 15–30% less expensive than national brands. They're often made in the same facilities with different labels. This switch can lead to monthly savings of $40–$60 for a family of four without sacrificing quality. You may not notice the difference—but your budget will.

How to Do It:

- Start with pantry basics: rice, pasta, canned beans, frozen veggies.

- Compare ingredients and nutrition labels to your usual brand.

- Taste-test as a family—make it fun!

- Stick to store brands for the items everyone approves.

- Save premium brands for special treats only.

---

4. Use a Running Grocery List

Summary:
Maintain a running grocery list in a central place at home. This prevents forgetfulness, reduces extra trips, and supports smart shopping habits.

Why This Works:
When families don't track what they run out of, they make multiple store trips and spend more with each one. A

running list helps consolidate your needs, avoid impulse buys, and make shopping more efficient. It also ensures you're not buying something you already have hidden in the pantry.

How to Do It:

- Keep a notepad or whiteboard on the fridge, or use a shared phone app.

- Train everyone to add things as soon as they run out.

- Before your weekly shop, review and organize the list.

- Check off items as you shop to stay focused and avoid distractions.

---

5. Skip Pre-Cut and Pre-Packaged Foods

Summary:
Avoid paying extra for chopped, peeled, or pre-packaged foods. Instead, prep at home for significant savings.

Why This Works:
You often pay 2–3 times more for convenience items like pre-cut fruit or snack-size packs. For example, a whole pineapple costs $3–$4, while the pre-cut version may be $7–$9. Cutting and portioning items at home only takes a few extra minutes and keeps more money in your pocket.

How to Do It:

- Buy whole fruits, cheese blocks, and large bags of snacks.

- Set aside time once a week to wash, chop, and store.

- Use reusable containers or snack bags.

- Get kids involved—assign simple snack-prep tasks.

- Create grab-and-go bins in your fridge and pantry.

2. UTILITIES & HOME EXPENSES

1. Adjust the Thermostat for Every Season

Summary:
Set your thermostat a few degrees lower in winter and higher in summer. It reduces heating and cooling bills without sacrificing comfort.

Why This Works:
Heating and cooling account for nearly half of home energy use. Lowering your thermostat by 1°C (2°F) in winter can save up to 5% on heating. A programmable thermostat or simple behaviour changes can save $150–$200 annually.

How to Do It:

- Aim for 68°F (20°C) in winter during the day, lower at night.

- In summer, raise to 76–78°F (24–26°C) when home.

- Use blankets, slippers, or ceiling fans as needed.

- Invest in a smart thermostat to auto-adjust for your schedule.

- Involve the whole family in being "temperature aware."

---

2. Switch to LED Light Bulbs

Summary:
Replace old incandescent or CFL bulbs with LED ones. They use less energy and last much longer, saving money on both usage and replacements.

Why This Works:
LEDs use up to 85% less electricity and last 15–25 times longer than traditional bulbs. A single bulb can save $50–$100 in electricity over its lifespan. Switching the whole home can create hundreds in long-term savings.

How to Do It:

- Start with the most-used bulbs: kitchen, living room, and entryway.

- Look for ENERGY STAR-rated bulbs for reliability.

- Choose warm or daylight tones depending on room use.

- Replace a few each month until the whole home is upgraded.

- Recycle old bulbs properly at a local depot.

---

3. Unplug Energy Vampires

Summary:
Unplug devices when they're not in use. Many electronics still draw power even when turned off—what's known as "phantom load."

Why This Works:
Phantom energy can account for 5–10% of your electricity bill. Devices like game consoles, coffee makers, printers, and chargers use electricity even when idle. Over time, this adds up to hundreds of kilowatt-hours.

How to Do It:

- Use power strips to group devices (TV, game system, speakers).

- Turn off or unplug chargers when not in use.

- Unplug small kitchen appliances between uses.

- Set reminders or create a "shutdown routine" for bedtime.

- Use smart plugs to automate energy savings.

---

4. Wash Laundry in Cold Water

Summary:
Switch to cold water for most laundry loads. It cleans just as well, saves energy, and protects your clothes.

Why This Works:
Nearly 90% of the energy in a wash cycle goes toward

heating water. Cold water detergents work well, even for stains. Cold water can save around $60–$80 annually for a family of four.

How to Do It:

- Set your washer's default to "cold wash."

- Use liquid detergent labelled for cold cycles.

- Save hot washes for towels or heavily soiled items.

- Combine full loads to reduce the number of cycles.

- Educate teens and kids about the new settings.

---

5. Take Shorter Showers

Summary:
Shortening showers by 2–3 minutes can dramatically reduce water and heating costs—especially in households with multiple family members.

Why This Works:
The average shower uses 2 gallons of water per minute. Cutting just 3 minutes off per person saves over 1,800 gallons of water and reduces water heating costs, potentially saving $100–$150 annually.

How to Do It:

- Use a waterproof timer or smart speaker in the bathroom.

- Make it a family challenge: 5-minute showers or less.

- Install low-flow showerheads to boost savings.

- Reward kids for hitting their time goals.

- Play a 3–5-minute song as their "shower soundtrack."

3. HOUSING & RENT/MORTGAGE

1. Ask for a Rent Renewal Discount

Summary:
When renewing your lease, ask your landlord for a rent reduction or to freeze the current rate. You could save hundreds yearly just by asking.

Why This Works:
Landlords often prefer good tenants over risking vacancy. If you've paid on time, kept the unit in good shape, or signed a longer lease, they may agree to hold or even reduce rent. It's easier and cheaper for them than finding new renters.

How to Do It:

- Ask 60–90 days before your lease ends.

- Mention your on-time payments and care for the unit.

- Offer a longer renewal term in exchange.

- Research average rents in your area to support your request.

- Be polite, reasonable, and ready to negotiate.

2. Refinance Your Mortgage Strategically

Summary:
Refinancing your mortgage at a lower interest rate or longer term can reduce monthly payments and increase financial flexibility.

Why This Works:
Even a 0.5–1% lower rate can save you hundreds per month or thousands over the life of the mortgage. Stretching your amortization slightly can also create breathing room, especially during tough times.

How to Do It:

- Check current rates from at least three lenders.

- Compare fixed vs. variable rates based on your risk tolerance.

- Run a mortgage calculator to estimate new payments.

- Talk to your existing lender about rate matching.

- Factor in fees—if the savings outweigh them, proceed.

---

3. House Hack: Rent Out a Room or Suite

Summary:
If your home has a spare room, basement, or garage apartment, renting it can offset your mortgage or utility costs.

Why This Works:
This is called "house hacking." Renting part of your space—even short-term—can generate $500–$1,000/month depending on your area. That income can go directly toward housing expenses.

How to Do It:

- Check local bylaws and your mortgage terms.

- Clean and furnish the space attractively.

- List on trusted platforms or through personal networks.

- Vet tenants carefully and set ground rules.

- Use rental income to pay down your mortgage or build savings.

---

4. Appeal Your Property Tax Assessment

Summary:
Homeowners can challenge high property tax assessments. If successful, your annual tax bill could drop—sometimes significantly.

Why This Works:
Municipal assessments aren't always accurate. You might be overpaying if your home is overvalued compared to similar properties. Appealing can reduce your taxable value and lower your yearly costs.

How to Do It:

- Review your latest property assessment letter.

- Compare with recent sales of similar homes in your area.

- Gather photos, data, or a realtor's opinion.

- File an appeal online or with your municipality's tax office.

- Follow deadlines carefully—most are within 60–90 days.

---

5. Bundle Home Insurance and Save

Summary:
Combine your home insurance with auto or life insurance to unlock discounts. Many providers offer 10–25% off for bundling policies.

Why This Works:
Insurance companies want your business. Bundling gives them more revenue and gives you more leverage for a discount. A family could easily save $200–$500 annually with a well-structured bundle.

How to Do It:

- Get quotes from your current insurer and one competitor.

- Ask for bundling incentives or multi-policy discounts.

- Compare not just price but coverage and deductibles.

- Set a calendar reminder to review your policy every year.

- Consider higher deductibles to lower premiums (if you have savings).

4. TRANSPORTATION

1. Bundle Your Car Trips for Savings

Summary:
Combine errands into fewer trips during the week. It saves fuel, reduces wear and tear, and makes your schedule more efficient.

Why This Works:
Cold starts use more fuel, and short trips strain your engine. Reducing trips can save 10–20% on fuel annually. Batching errands lowers gas costs and time spent driving for families juggling work, school, and sports.

How to Do It:

- Create a weekly "errand day" with a looped route.

- Group visits to stores and appointments by location.

- Use your phone's map app to plan the most efficient order.

- Keep a family whiteboard or app to log weekly needs.

- Fill your tank once a week to avoid midweek detours.

2. Use Cruise Control on Highways

Summary:
Cruise control helps maintain a steady highway speed, improving fuel efficiency and lowering stress during long drives.

Why This Works:
Frequent speed changes use more fuel. Cruise control can improve mileage by up to 7% on flat highways. It also reduces speeding and makes driving more relaxing—especially helpful for weekend family trips.

How to Do It:

- Use cruise control on open roads, not in traffic.

- Set speed 5–10 km/h below the limit to save fuel.

- Turn off cruise control in the rain or on hilly terrain.

- Teach teens how to use it safely and when to avoid it.

- Pair with "eco" driving mode if your car has one.

---

3. Pump Tires to the Right Pressure

Summary:
Check and inflate your tires monthly. Proper tire pressure improves gas mileage and helps tires last longer.

Why This Works:
Under-inflated tires reduce fuel efficiency by up to 3%. Most families earn $60–$90 a year in gas. They also wear

unevenly and shorten tire life. Properly inflating them is one of the easiest, most overlooked car-care tips.

How to Do It:

- Check pressure monthly with a $10 tire gauge.

- Find the correct PSI on a sticker on the driver's door.

- Fill up at free air stations at gas stations.

- Re-check before long trips or in extreme temperatures.

- Teach older kids to help as part of vehicle care.

---

4. Share School Drop-Offs with Neighbors

Summary:
Start or join a carpool for school runs. It saves gas, reduces emissions, and gives parents a needed break.

Why This Works:
If four families each take one school morning, you cut your car use by 75%. It also helps build community and cuts traffic at school entrances. Less idling means less fuel burned and fewer emissions.

How to Do It:

- Ask trusted neighbours or friends at school.

- Create a shared calendar or WhatsApp group.

- Agree on pickup spots, safety rules, and timing.

- Keep emergency contacts for each child in the car.

- Celebrate with coffee on your "off days."

---

5. Opt for Public Transit or Monthly Passes

Summary:
When possible, use public transportation. Monthly passes are often cheaper than gas and parking—especially for regular commutes.

Why This Works:
Transit eliminates fuel, parking, and maintenance costs. A $135 monthly pass might replace $300–$400 car expenses. It also offers predictability and frees time for reading, podcasts, or work.

How to Do It:

- Look up routes to your workplace, school, or gym.

- Calculate monthly car costs and compare with pass price.

- Start with 1–2 days per week and increase gradually.

- Use a transit card app to track usage.

- Walk or bike the last leg to stay active.

5. CHILDCARE & EDUCATION

1. Use Free Educational Apps and Libraries

Summary:
Supplement school learning at home with free apps and local libraries. It supports your child's growth while saving on books and pricey programs.

Why This Works:
Apps like Khan Academy, Duolingo, and Epic! Offer quality learning for free. Libraries provide access to homework help, workshops, and digital learning—all at no cost. These tools support academic success and help reduce tutoring or material expenses.

How to Do It:

- Visit your local library to explore free resources.

- Sign up for digital access to eBooks and audiobooks.

- Choose 1–2 age-appropriate apps for your kids.

- Set learning goals with your child (e.g., 15 minutes/day).

- Use screen time intentionally with learning apps instead of games.

---

2. Pack School Lunches in Bulk

Summary:
Packing school lunches in weekly batches saves money and

reduces waste compared to daily purchases or convenience options.

Why This Works:
Buying school lunches daily can cost $4–$10 per child. Homemade lunches average $2–$3. Packing in bulk keeps costs low and ensures kids eat healthier. Prepping five lunches simultaneously saves time during busy mornings.

How to Do It:

- Plan a simple lunch menu for the week.

- Use bento boxes or reusable containers.

- Prep sandwiches, fruits, and snacks on Sunday night.

- Freeze portions if needed to keep them fresh.

- Let kids help pack to ensure they'll eat it!

---

3. Share Childcare with Trusted Families

Summary:
Coordinate with other parents to alternate childcare days. It cuts babysitting or after-school costs without sacrificing safety or structure.

Why This Works:
Hiring babysitters regularly adds up. Sharing care with trusted families reduces your expenses and builds community. Even 1–2 shared days weekly can save $150–$300 per month, especially for preschool or early elementary kids.

How to Do It:

- Connect with other parents at school or daycare.

- Start with one test day to build trust.

- Align schedules, house rules, and activities.

- Keep communication open with a shared calendar.

- Offer snacks, homework time, and play in a safe space.

---

4. Shop School Supplies Strategically

Summary:
Buy school supplies during seasonal sales, in bulk, or at discount stores. Plan your purchases instead of last-minute panic shopping.

Why This Works:
Late shopping leads to premium prices. Bulk buys from dollar stores or mid-summer sales can cut costs by 30–50%. You'll also avoid duplicate purchases when you reuse last year's leftovers.

How to Do It:

- Take inventory of what you already have at home.

- Buy during back-to-school promotions (July–August).

- Stock up on year-round basics (notebooks, glue sticks).

- Set a small budget and stick to it.

- Use coupons or price-match at big-box stores.

---

5. Use Government Subsidies and Tax Credits

Summary:
Explore national, regional, or local programs that offer financial support for childcare, education, or family expenses. Many families qualify without realizing it.

Why This Works:
Governments often provide monthly payments, tax credits, or matching grants to help with the cost of raising children. Though sometimes modest, these benefits can add up to thousands per year when combined, offering real relief for your household budget.

How to Do It:

- Visit your country's official tax or social services website to see what programs you qualify for.

- Look for support related to childcare, after-school programs, school supplies, or tuition.

- Save and submit receipts for child-related expenses when filing your taxes.

- Ask your accountant or a tax advisor about national or local family benefit programs.

- Open education savings accounts (e.g., 529 Plan in the U.S., matched savings in the U.K. or elsewhere) to receive government contributions.

6. HEALTH & WELLNESS

1. Choose Generic Medications When Possible

Summary:
Ask your pharmacist for the generic version of prescriptions. They offer the same health benefits at a significantly lower cost.

Why This Works:
Generic drugs are regulated to be as effective as name brands but can cost up to 85% less. This can mean hundreds of dollars saved annually—without sacrificing quality for recurring prescriptions or over-the-counter meds.

How to Do It:

- Ask your doctor to prescribe the generic version by default.

- Confirm availability at the pharmacy—some require a request.

- Compare prices at different pharmacies using apps like GoodRx (U.S.) or local flyers.

- Buy in bulk if you have ongoing prescriptions.

- Review your family's recurring medications annually.

---

2. Maximize Your Health Benefits Plan

Summary:
Fully use your employer or private health plan each year.

Many families miss out on covered services like massage, physio, or dental care.

Why This Works:
Unused benefits are lost and not rolled over. If your plan covers $500/year for physiotherapy, that's like leaving $500 on the table. Using these services can prevent more enormous medical bills later.

How to Do It:

- Review your plan at the beginning of the year.

- Book check-ups, cleanings, or preventive visits in advance.

- Ask your provider what's covered per person.

- Track what you've used mid-year to avoid rushing in December.

- Coordinate with your partner's plan if dual coverage exists.

---

3. Walk or Bike Instead of Driving

Summary:
Replace short drives with walking or biking. It boosts your family's fitness and cuts transportation and health-related expenses.

Why This Works:
Exercise reduces the risk of chronic illnesses and can lower future medical costs. Swapping a car for legs saves gas and

parking fees. Kids also learn healthy habits that stick into adulthood.

How to Do It:

- Choose one regular errand to walk to each week.

- Walk the kids to school a few days a week.

- Keep shoes, helmets, and bikes ready near the door.

- Start a family walking challenge with small rewards.

- Bundle walking with quality family time.

---

4. Use Community Fitness Programs

Summary:
Join free or low-cost fitness classes at community centers or local parks instead of pricey gym memberships.

Why This Works:
Many cities offer yoga, Zumba, swimming, or kids' sports at a fraction of the cost of private gyms. These programs help you stay active as a family without overspending.

How to Do It:

- Check your local municipal website or rec center.

- Look for programs labelled "free" or "subsidized."

- Register early—spots can fill up quickly.

- Encourage kids to try new activities each season.

- Invite a neighbour or friend to keep you motivated.

---

5. Meal Prep for Better Nutrition and Savings

Summary:
Healthy eating starts at home. Planning and prepping meals cuts fast food costs and improves long-term wellness.

Why This Works:
Families spend more on takeout when unprepared. Healthy home meals can reduce the risk of diet-related diseases. You'll also minimize grocery waste and stress at dinnertime.

How to Do It:

- Plan five simple meals each week.

- Prep ingredients on Sundays—chop, portion, or cook ahead.

- Pack healthy lunches to avoid cafeteria or takeout costs.

- Get kids involved in choosing or cooking meals.

- Freeze leftovers for busy days.

7. CLOTHING & PERSONAL ITEMS

1. Shop End-of-Season Clearance Racks

Summary:
Buy clothes at the end of each season for the following year. You'll find quality items for 50–70% less than peak prices.

Why This Works:
Retailers clear inventory after each season. Kids grow fast, but sizing up ensures next year's fit. You'll avoid paying full price and beat the last-minute scramble in high-demand months.

How to Do It:

- Buy winter clothes in March and summer in August.

- Choose timeless basics that won't go out of style.

- Size up for kids to account for growth.

- Set a clothing budget per child for off-season deals.

- Store finds in a labelled bin until needed.

---

2. Buy Gently Used from Thrift or Online

Summary:
Shop secondhand for clothes, accessories, and personal items in good condition. Many look new and cost a fraction of retail.

Why This Works:
Kids wear clothes for only a season or two. Thrift stores,

online marketplaces, and consignment sales offer huge discounts—often 70–90% off. You'll stretch your budget and reduce waste.

How to Do It:

- Try local thrift stores, Facebook Marketplace, or Poshmark.

- Search by size and condition ("like new" or "NWT").

- Wash items thoroughly and inspect for damage.

- Sell your kids' old clothes to fund the next batch.

- Make thrifting a family outing—it's fun!

---

3. Embrace Hand-Me-Downs Proudly

Summary:
Use hand-me-downs from siblings, cousins, or friends. It saves money and reduces environmental impact.

Why This Works:
Most clothes don't get worn out—kids just outgrow them. Sharing clothes between families creates a low-cost, high-trust supply chain. It's budget-friendly and sustainable.

How to Do It:

- Ask friends or family with older kids about swaps.

- Join local parent groups or "Buy Nothing" networks.

- Wash and store outgrown clothes neatly for future use.

- Organize hand-me-down bins by size/season.

- Say thank you with a small gesture or return items.

---

4. Simplify Your Personal Grooming Routine

Summary:
Cut back on high-end grooming products or frequent salon visits. Focus on essential tools and routines that work for your lifestyle.

Why This Works:
Many families spend hundreds annually on name-brand items, haircuts, or skin products that aren't necessary. Streamlining routines saves time and serious money—without sacrificing cleanliness or self-care.

How to Do It:

- Choose multipurpose products (e.g., shampoo + body wash).

- Try at-home trims with YouTube tutorials.

- Limit haircuts to every 8–12 weeks, not 4–6.

- Simplify skincare to just cleanser and moisturizer.

- Track your grooming spending for 1–2 months.

---

5. Host or Attend a Clothing Swap Event

Summary:
Organize or join a clothing swap in your community. Everyone brings outgrown or unused items to exchange.

Why This Works:
Swaps create a win-win: you declutter and get new clothes—for free. Families save money and build community. It's especially great for kids, maternity wear, and seasonal gear.

How to Do It:

- Coordinate with school, daycare, or neighbourhood groups.

- Sort clothes by size/gender for easier browsing.

- Invite participants to bring clean, gently used items.

- Set up tables and "shop" for what you need.

- Donate leftovers to a local shelter.

8. ENTERTAINMENT & FAMILY ACTIVITIES

1. Schedule a Weekly Family Game Night

Summary:
Create a dedicated evening for board games or card games. It's a low-cost way to bond, laugh, and build family traditions.

Why This Works:
Game nights cost nothing once you own a few games. They encourage interaction, reduce screen time, and create

memories. You'll spend less on outings while still connecting deeply at home.

How to Do It:

- Choose one evening a week (e.g., Fridays).

- Rotate who picks the game each week.

- Start with what you already have—Uno, Jenga, puzzles.

- Borrow or swap games with friends for variety.

- Add homemade snacks for extra fun.

---

2. Explore Free Library Events and Resources

Summary:
Your local library offers more than books—think free passes, classes, story times, and maker spaces for all ages.

Why This Works:
Libraries often provide entertainment alternatives that would otherwise cost money—movies, tutoring, events, and even museum passes. Families can save hundreds annually just by participating regularly.

How to Do It:

- Check your library's online calendar weekly.

- Register early for popular events or clubs.

- Borrow books, audiobooks, and DVDs instead of buying.

- Ask about free or discounted passes to local attractions.

- Make library visits a family ritual.

---

3. Host Potluck Parties with Friends

Summary:
Instead of expensive dinners out, host simple potlucks. Everyone brings something, and kids get to socialize without added cost.

Why This Works:
Potlucks slash the cost of entertaining. You get quality time with friends, various food, and no restaurant bill or tip. Plus, kids love playing with friends at home.

How to Do It:

- Invite 1–3 families for a casual evening.

- Assign dishes: one brings dessert, another a main.

- Rotate hosts to share the effort.

- Include music, games, or outdoor fun.

- Set a budget-friendly theme if desired.

---

4. Create a DIY Movie Night at Home

Summary:
Transform your living room into a "home theatre" with snacks and streaming. It's cheaper and cozier than going out.

Why This Works:
Movie tickets, snacks, and parking can cost $60+ for a family. At home, you control the experience and cost. Plus, kids can pause for bathroom breaks and wear pajamas!

How to Do It:

- Choose a movie and make a "ticket" for each person.

- Pop your own popcorn and set out treats.

- Dim the lights and cozy up with blankets.

- Rotate who picks the movie each week.

- Use streaming services or library DVDs.

---

5. Rotate Streaming Subscriptions

Summary:
Use one streaming service at a time. Rotate monthly instead of paying for several at once.

Why This Works:
Many families subscribe to 3–5 services but only use one regularly. Cancelling and rotating saves $20–50/month while offering new content throughout the year.

How to Do It:

- List the services your family uses.

- Choose one per month (e.g., Disney+ in April, Netflix in May).

- Cancel others before the billing cycle ends.

- Set a calendar reminder to switch.

- Use free trials to test before paying.

9. GIFTS, HOLIDAYS & CELEBRATIONS

1. Set a Celebration Budget in Advance

Summary:
Decide on your total budget for holidays or parties before planning. It helps prioritize what matters and prevents surprise spending.

Why This Works:
Setting a budget early avoids overspending on decorations, food, or gifts out of impulse or guilt. It forces smarter choices and keeps the focus on meaningful moments, not just stuff.

How to Do It:

- Choose your maximum budget for the occasion.

- Break it down into categories: food, gifts, decor.

- Use cash or prepaid cards to stay on track.

- Track spending in a simple notebook or app.

- Involve older kids in the planning—it teaches financial skills.

---

2. Give DIY or Personalized Gifts

Summary:
Make gifts at home or personalize inexpensive items. They're more meaningful—and often more appreciated—than pricey store-bought ones.

Why This Works:
DIY gifts show care and creativity. Handmade cards, baked goods, or photo books cost little but feel special. Kids can also join the fun, adding their personal touch.

How to Do It:

- Use Pinterest or YouTube for simple DIY gift ideas.

- Bake cookies, craft ornaments, or frame a favourite photo.

- Personalize items with names or shared memories.

- Stock up on craft supplies during sales.

- Wrap with recycled paper or fabric for charm and savings.

---

3. Host Potluck Celebrations

Summary:
Share the cost and effort of hosting by asking guests to

bring a dish. It lowers expenses and creates a community vibe.

Why This Works:
Food is the most significant cost of hosting. Potlucks cut this significantly while offering variety and engaging everyone in the celebration. It also reduces stress on the host.

How to Do It:

- Send invites with a sign-up sheet or dish suggestion.

- Provide the main dish, drinks, or dessert.

- Ask about allergies to plan inclusively.

- Use disposable or borrowed serving ware to simplify cleanup.

- Offer guests takeaway containers to avoid waste.

---

4. Create a Gift Closet or Bin

Summary:
Buy versatile gifts and supplies year-round during sales. Store them in a bin for birthdays, teacher gifts, or holidays.

Why This Works:
Last-minute gifts cost more. Stocking up during clearance events gives you low-cost options on hand. You avoid the store rush and stress of shopping under pressure.

How to Do It:

- Designate a closet shelf or bin for gifts and cards.

- Buy classic toys, candles, books, or puzzles on sale.

- Keep extra wrapping paper, tape, and bags.

- Label items by recipient type (e.g., "adult," "child," "teacher").

- Check your bin before every event or invitation.

---

5. Reuse and Refresh Decorations

Summary:
Store and reuse holiday or party decorations creatively. Add new touches for a fresh feel without starting from scratch.

Why This Works:
Decor can eat up a big chunk of holiday spending. Reusing what you already own—and creatively updating it—can save you hundreds over the years while still feeling festive.

How to Do It:

- Pack decorations by theme and label bins.

- Use neutral or multi-use items (like string lights or tablecloths).

- Add new accents (like ribbons or signs) to refresh.

- Store gently to extend their lifespan.

- Involve kids in decorating—it boosts fun and saves on labour.

10. DEBT, BANKING & SUBSCRIPTIONS

1. Cancel Unused Subscriptions Today

Summary:
Review your bank and credit card statements for recurring subscriptions you forgot about or no longer use—and cancel them immediately.

Why This Works:
It's common to pay for 5–10 digital services monthly. Even $10/month adds up to $120/year. Cutting just 2–3 of these frees up real money with zero lifestyle impact.

How to Do It:

- Log into your bank/credit card account.

- Highlight all monthly recurring charges.

- Cancel anything unused or duplicated (music, streaming, cloud storage).

- Use a cancellation tracking app if needed.

- Repeat this review every 3–4 months.

---

2. Switch to a No-Fee or Low-Fee Bank

Summary:
If your current bank charges you monthly fees or transaction costs, consider switching to one that doesn't—or offers cash-back perks.

Why This Works:
Banking fees can quietly eat $180+ per year. Many online banks or credit unions offer free accounts with fewer restrictions, better interest, and modern features.

How to Do It:

- Compare your current fees to alternatives (Tangerine, Simplii, EQ, etc.).

- Look for no-fee chequing and free Interac e-transfers.

- Open your new account and set up auto-deposit.

- Switch bill payments and close the old account.

- Ask your bank to waive fees—you might get a deal.

---

3. Use the Snowball Method to Pay Off Debt

Summary:
List your debts from smallest to largest. Pay off the smallest first while making minimums on the rest. Then move on to the next.

Why This Works:
The snowball method builds momentum and motivation. Each paid-off debt is a win, which increases confidence and creates breathing room in your budget.

How to Do It:

- List all debts: amount, interest rate, minimum payment.

- Focus all extra funds on the smallest balance.

- Once paid, roll that payment into the next smallest.

- Celebrate each milestone.

- Avoid adding new debt during the process.

---

4. Call to Lower Your Interest Rate

Summary:
Call your credit card company and ask for a lower interest rate. It can dramatically reduce the cost of carrying a balance.

Why This Works:
Many card issuers will reduce your APR if you've been a loyal customer. Even a 3–5% drop in interest can save hundreds yearly on large balances.

How to Do It:

- Call the number on the back of your card.

- Politely request a lower interest rate due to your history.

- Be prepared to mention competitors or balance transfer offers.

- Document the outcome.

- Repeat annually or if your credit score improves.

---

5. Consolidate Debt for Simpler Payments

Summary:
If you have multiple debts, combine them into one lower-interest loan. It reduces monthly stress and often saves on interest.

Why This Works:
Debt consolidation turns chaos into clarity. With one predictable monthly payment and lower interest, it's easier to budget and avoid missed payments or penalties.

How to Do It:

- Add up all your non-mortgage debt.

- Check bank or credit union options for personal loans.

- Compare interest rates and fees carefully.

- Apply only if the new rate is lower than your current average.

- Stop using old credit lines after consolidation.

11. EMERGENCY PREPAREDNESS & INSURANCE

1. Establish a Dedicated Emergency Fund

Summary: Create a savings account for unforeseen expenses to cover 3–6 months' living costs.

Why This Works: An emergency fund acts as a financial buffer, reducing the need to rely on high-interest loans or credit cards during a crisis.

How to Do It:

- Open a separate high-interest savings account.

- Automate monthly transfers, even if modest.

- Use windfalls like tax refunds to boost the fund.

- Regularly review and adjust contributions as finances allow.

---

2. Conduct Annual Insurance Policy Reviews

Summary: Assess your insurance coverage yearly to ensure it aligns with current needs and circumstances.

Why This Works: Changes like home renovations, new family members, or significant purchases can alter coverage requirements. Regular reviews prevent overpaying or being underinsured.

How to Do It:

- Schedule a yearly meeting with your insurance advisor.

- Update policies to reflect recent life changes.

- Compare premiums and coverage with other providers.

- Ensure beneficiaries and contact information are current.

---

3. Bundle Insurance Policies for Discounts

Summary: Combine multiple insurance policies (e.g., home and auto) with a single provider to qualify for bundling discounts.

Why This Works: Insurers often offer reduced rates for customers holding multiple policies, leading to significant savings.

How to Do It:

- Inquire your current insurer about bundling options.

- Compare bundled rates among different providers.

- Evaluate the overall coverage to ensure it meets all needs.

- Be mindful of policy terms and potential penalties for change.

---

4. Increase Deductibles to Lower Premiums

Summary: Opt for higher deductibles on insurance policies to reduce monthly premium costs.

Why This Works: Higher deductibles typically result in lower premiums, offering savings over time, provided you have funds set aside to cover the deductible if needed.

How to Do It:

- Assess your financial ability to cover higher deductibles.

- Consult with your insurance provider about premium reductions.

- Adjust your emergency fund to accommodate potential deductible expenses.

- Ensure the deductible increase doesn't exceed your risk comfort level.

---

5. Eliminate Redundant or Unnecessary Coverage

Summary: Review and remove insurance coverage that no longer serves your current situation or duplicates other policies.

Why This Works: Paying for unnecessary coverage is a financial drain. Streamlining policies ensures you're only paying for what you truly need.

How to Do It:

- List all active insurance policies and their coverage.

- Identify overlaps or outdated policies.

- Consult with your insurance advisor before making changes.

- Redirect savings from cancelled policies to other financial priorities.

12. WORK & SIDE INCOME

1. Sell Unused Items for Quick Cash

Summary:
Declutter your home and turn forgotten stuff into income. Sell items online, at yard sales, or through local marketplaces.

Why This Works:
Most households have around $300–$1,000 worth of unused items. Selling them clears space, earns quick money, and kick-starts saving goals.

How to Do It:

- Walk through each room with a "sell or keep" box.

- Gather toys, clothes, electronics, tools, or decor.

- Use Facebook Marketplace, Kijiji, or a garage sale.

- Take clear photos and write honest descriptions.

- Put profits into emergency savings or debt payments.

---

2. Turn a Hobby Into Side Income

Summary:
Use your skills—like baking, photography, or tutoring—to offer services or products others will gladly pay for.

Why This Works:
Doing what you enjoy is sustainable and motivating.

Hobbies often solve real needs for others, allowing you to earn extra income with little upfront cost.

How to Do It:

- Identify what people often ask you for help with.

- Start small—bake for friends, tutor one student, offer a craft.

- Advertise locally or on social media.

- Set fair prices based on time and materials.

- Track all income and expenses for tax purposes.

---

3. Save on Work Lunches by Meal Prepping

Summary:
Bringing homemade meals saves $50–$100 per month. It's healthier, cheaper, and avoids the temptation of daily takeout.

Why This Works:
Even a $10 lunch 3x/week adds up to $120/month. Prepping meals at home costs a fraction and builds consistent savings with minimal effort.

How to Do It:

- Set aside one hour on Sunday to prep lunches.

- Cook in bulk (soups, rice bowls, pasta).

- Store in portioned containers for grab-and-go.

- Include snacks and drinks to avoid vending machines.

- Make it a family habit—kids can prep, too.

---

4. Cut Commuting Costs with Remote Days

Summary:
If your job allows, working from home just 1–2 days a week can reduce gas, parking, and wear on your vehicle.

Why This Works:
Reducing commute days reduces transportation costs by up to 40% and gives back weekly hours. That's a win for your budget and your well-being.

How to Do It:

- Track what your commute costs per day.

- Talk to your employer about flexible remote options.

- Schedule deep-focus tasks for your at-home days.

- Use saved time for rest or side income activities.

- Reevaluate monthly for long-term balance.

---

5. Start a Family Micro-Business

Summary:
Involve your kids in a simple side business—like lemonade stands, dog walking, or art sales. It teaches entrepreneurship and earns income.

Why This Works:
Kids learn responsibility, math, and money management while contributing to family savings. These experiences build lifelong confidence and skills.

How to Do It:

- Brainstorm ideas your child is excited about.

- Guide them to set prices and make a sign or flyer.

- Help with basic setup, but let them take the lead.

- Celebrate their earnings—save, spend, and give portions.

- Expand if it works—word of mouth spreads fast!

13. ENVIRONMENTAL SAVINGS (GREEN LIVING)

1. Switch to Reusable Kitchen Essentials

Summary:
Replace disposable items like paper towels, plastic wrap, and napkins with reusable alternatives to cut waste and recurring costs.

Why This Works:
The average family spends $100–$200 per year on

disposables. Reusable clothes and containers could last years, reduce trash and offer long-term savings.

How to Do It:

- Replace paper towels with washable cloths or rags.

- Use beeswax wraps or containers instead of plastic wrap.

- Store reusable napkins in an easy-access drawer.

- Wash weekly with regular laundry.

- Buy once, save for years.

---

2. Embrace Line-Drying Your Laundry

Summary:
Use a clothesline or drying rack instead of the dryer when possible. It reduces electricity use and extends the life of your clothes.

Why This Works:
Dryers are energy hogs. Air-drying saves up to $100/year and reduces wear and tear on fabrics—especially helpful for kids' clothes.

How to Do It:

- Install an indoor rack or outdoor line.

- Hang heavier items first, then lighter ones.

- Dry during sunny or breezy parts of the day.

- Use hangers to reduce wrinkles and folding.

- Make it a routine, not a chore.

---

3. Start Composting to Cut Waste

Summary:
Compost food scraps instead of tossing them in the trash. It reduces landfill waste and turns leftovers into garden gold.

Why This Works:
Composting cuts your garbage volume, saving on trash bags and city fees. It also improves soil, reducing the need for fertilizers or lawn treatments.

How to Do It:

- Set up a small bin on your kitchen counter.

- Collect fruit, veggie peels, coffee grounds, and eggshells.

- Empty into an outdoor compost bin or pile.

- Stir occasionally to speed breakdown.

- Use compost for houseplants or garden beds.

---

4. Switch to LED Bulbs Throughout the House

Summary:
Replace traditional incandescent or CFL bulbs with LED alternatives for significant energy savings and less frequent replacement.

Why This Works:
LEDs use up to 85% less energy and last 15–20 times longer. Swapping 10 bulbs can save around $100–$150 per year.

How to Do It:

- Make a list of all bulbs in your home.

- Replace the most-used lights first (kitchen, bathroom, hallways).

- Look for ENERGY STAR-rated LEDs.

- Choose soft white or daylight tones for comfort.

- Track savings on your utility bill.

---

5. Use a Refillable Water Bottle

Summary:
Avoid single-use plastic bottles by giving each family member a refillable water bottle for school, work, and outings.

Why This Works:
Bottled water is 300–2,000 times more expensive than tap

water. A $20 bottle pays for itself in weeks and keeps plastic out of landfills.

How to Do It:

- Choose durable, BPA-free bottles with fun colours or themes.

- Keep them near keys or the fridge for easy grab-and-go.

- Use tap or filtered water at home.

- Wash daily with a bottle brush.

- Celebrate "zero plastic" days with your kids.

14. TECHNOLOGY & DEVICES

1. Buy Refurbished or Gently Used Tech

Summary:
Before buying new, check for certified refurbished or pre-owned phones, tablets, or laptops. You'll get a like-new function at a fraction of the cost.

Why This Works:
Brand-new tech depreciates fast. Refurbished models often cost 30–50% less, include warranties, and function nearly identically to new models.

How to Do It:

- Check trusted retailers like Apple Refurbished, Best Buy, or Back Market.

- Look for "certified refurbished" with at least 90-day warranties.

- Compare specs—often, last year's model is more than enough.

- Save the difference for future upgrades.

---

2. Share a Family Cell Plan

Summary:
Combine phone lines into one family plan to cut your monthly bill and simplify management.

Why This Works:
Family plans often offer multi-line discounts, shared data, and better deals on new devices. Splitting individual lines can cost 25–40% more per month.

How to Do It:

- Compare plans from your provider vs. competitors.

- Bundle multiple family members under one account.

- Choose shared data with alerts to avoid overages.

- Revisit the plan annually as needs change.

---

3. Delay Device Upgrades Strategically

Summary:
Resist upgrading phones or gadgets every 1–2 years unless

necessary. Stretching each device's life saves hundreds annually.

Why This Works:
Most phones and laptops last 3–5 years with proper care. Upgrading only when performance drops prevents wasteful spending on minor improvements.

How to Do It:

- Protect devices with good cases and screen protectors.

- Replace batteries or storage before replacing the whole device.

- Skip upgrade promos unless your current device is broken.

- Reframe newer as "nice to have," not "need to have."

---

4. Limit In-App Purchases with Controls

Summary:
Set parental controls to block or require approval for all in-app purchases—especially on games, entertainment, or kids' apps.

Why This Works:
In-app spending can sneak up on families. Without realizing it, a few $3–$10 weekly charges add up to hundreds per year.

How to Do It:

- Enable parental controls on each child's device.

- Require password or fingerprint to approve purchases.

- Turn off 1-click payment features.

- Set app-store spending limits or use gift cards for budgeted spending.

---

5. Use Free or Discounted Software Alternatives

Summary:
Instead of expensive programs, explore free or discounted software for school, work, and creativity.

Why This Works:
Many paid tools have free or open-source equivalents (e.g., LibreOffice, Canva, GIMP, Google Docs). Switching saves money with little trade-off in quality.

How to Do It:

- Identify your top 3 most-used tools.

- Search for free versions or alternatives.

- Ask your child's school or employer for licensed discounts.

- Uninstall unused software to avoid clutter and fees.

15. INSURANCE OPTIMIZATION (BEYOND HOME & AUTO)

1. Compare Term Life Insurance Options Every Few Years

Summary:
If it's been a while, revisit your life insurance. Rates drop as the market changes or your health improves.

Why This Works:
Many people stick with their first policy without comparison. But just like refinancing a mortgage, switching term policies can reduce premiums by 10–30%.

How to Do It:

- Request updated quotes from 2–3 providers.

- Use an online broker to save time.

- Compare not just cost but length and benefits.

- Lock in fixed rates while you're healthy.

- Cancel old policies only after new ones are active.

---

2. Opt for Term Life Over Whole Life

Summary:
Choose term life insurance to get higher coverage for a lower premium—especially while your kids are still financially dependent.

Why This Works:
Term life costs far less than whole life. You can invest the difference yourself while still covering your family's needs.

How to Do It:

- Decide how many years of coverage you need (e.g. until kids finish school).

- Calculate the amount to cover debts, education, and income replacement.

- Choose a reputable insurer offering low rates for 20–30 year terms.

- Reassess after significant life events.

---

3. Use Your Workplace Benefits First

Summary:
Maximize dental, vision, and life insurance offered through your employer—it's often cheaper than buying your own policy.

Why This Works:
Group benefits typically cost less and include built-in subsidies. You're already paying for them—make the most of what's available.

How to Do It:

- Review your employee benefits booklet annually.

- Use preventive dental and vision visits to avoid higher costs later.

- Opt into extra coverage if rates are competitive.

- Combine with a spouse's plan for better reimbursement.

---

4. Bundle Health, Life & Travel with One Provider

Summary:
Group multiple personal policies—like dental, life, and travel insurance—with the same provider to access discounts and streamline management.

Why This Works:
Insurers often reward loyalty and multi-policy holders with 5–15% savings. It also reduces paperwork and renewal stress.

How to Do It:

- List your existing policies and providers.

- Get quotes from insurers offering multi-policy discounts.

- Ensure you're not duplicating coverage.

- Consolidate only if it improves value and terms.

---

5. Only Buy What You Need Today

Summary:
Avoid paying for features or riders that don't apply to your current life stage or income level.

Why This Works:
Extra bells and whistles (like child riders or hospital cash) can quietly add up. Tailoring your policy saves money and focuses protection where it matters.

How to Do It:

- Review optional add-ons with a broker.

- Ask: "What real risk am I covering here?"

- Cancel unneeded riders after kids grow or debts shrink.

- Keep policies lean and adjustable.

16. HOUSEHOLD SUPPLIES & CLEANING

1. Make Your Own All-Purpose Cleaner

Summary:
Skip pricey name-brand sprays. Mix basic ingredients at home to create a safe, effective, all-purpose cleaner.

Why This Works:
DIY cleaners cost just pennies per bottle. Vinegar, baking soda, and lemon juice can clean most surfaces while eliminating harsh chemicals.

How to Do It:

- Mix 1 cup white vinegar + 1 cup water in a spray bottle.

- Add a few drops of essential oil (like lemon or lavender).

- Use on countertops, windows, and bathroom surfaces.

- Label the bottle and keep it in your cleaning caddy.

- Refill as needed—easy and eco-friendly.

---

2. Replace Paper Towels with Reusable Clothes

Summary:
Stop buying paper towels every few weeks. Use reusable clothes or cut-up t-shirts instead.

Why This Works:
Families spend $100+ per year on paper towels. Reusables last for years, create less waste and are just as effective.

How to Do It:

- Buy a stack of microfiber cloths or cut old towels.

- Store them in a basket under the sink.

- Use for spills, dusting, and countertops.

- Toss used ones into a "dirty bin" for weekly laundry.

- Save paper towels for only greasy or guest uses.

3. Buy Cleaning Products in Bulk

Summary:
Purchase supplies in larger quantities of detergent, soap, and toilet paper to reduce cost per use and trips to the store.

Why This Works:
Bulk buying can save 20–40% compared to smaller packaging. Fewer trips also reduce impulse spending.

How to Do It:

- Choose warehouse stores or online bulk suppliers.

- Stick to non-perishables you use regularly.

- Store extras in a labelled closet bin.

- Keep one bottle in use and refill from the big jug.

- Share a membership with friends to split the cost.

4. Simplify with Fewer Specialized Products

Summary:
You don't need a different cleaner for every room. Use versatile products that clean multiple surfaces.

Why This Works:
Specialty items cost more and clutter your cabinets. Multi-use products reduce waste, decision fatigue, and spending.

How to Do It:

- Choose one good all-purpose cleaner and one disinfectant.

- Test them in your bathroom, kitchen, and floors.

- Eliminate duplicates over time.

- Track what truly gets used.

- Make a minimalist list before you restock.

---

5. Use Half the Recommended Detergent

Summary:
Cut your laundry or dish detergent usage in half. Most machines work just as well with less.

Why This Works:
Manufacturers recommend more than necessary to sell faster. Using half extends your supply and avoids soap buildup.

How to Do It:

- Mark a lower fill line on your detergent cap.

- Try half-loads and track cleaning results.

- Use warm—not hot—water to boost cleaning.

- Clean your machine filter regularly for efficiency.

- Adjust up only if needed.

17. SUBSCRIPTIONS & MEMBERSHIPS

1. Cancel What You're Not Using Monthly

Summary:
Review all active subscriptions—streaming, gyms, kids' boxes—every month and cancel anything underused or forgotten.

Why This Works:
Families often pay $50–$100/month for services no one's using. Regular check-ins help you spend intentionally and free up cash flow.

How to Do It:

- Check your credit card/bank for recurring charges.

- Ask: "Have we used this in the last 30 days?"

- Cancel unused trials before they convert.

- Set a reminder to repeat this every month.

- Celebrate each cancellation as a win.

---

2. Rotate Streaming Services One at a Time

Summary:
Instead of paying for multiple streaming platforms at once, subscribe to one or two per month, then switch.

Why This Works:
You likely only watch shows on one or two platforms

regularly. Rotating saves $15–$30/month with zero entertainment loss.

How to Do It:

- Create a family watch list by platform.

- Pause unused subscriptions in app settings.

- Switch services monthly or seasonally.

- Use free trials to bridge the gap.

- Talk with kids about "TV time budgeting."

---

3. Share Subscriptions Within Your Household

Summary:
Many services allow family sharing—ensure you're not unnecessarily paying for separate accounts.

Why This Works:
Streaming, music, and cloud storage platforms offer family plans that save 25–50% compared to individual accounts.

How to Do It:

- Check your provider's "Family" or "Household" settings.

- Merge accounts under one bill.

- Use individual profiles for personalization.

- Cap how many users/devices are allowed.

- Review usage and split costs if needed.

---

4. Set Calendar Reminders for Free Trials

Summary:
Before starting any free trial, create a calendar alert 1–2 days before it expires to cancel if not needed.

Why This Works:
Many families forget to cancel, leading to surprise charges. A 30-second reminder saves $10–$100+ across multiple services.

How to Do It:

- Add a calendar event when starting a free trial.

- Include login details and cancel instructions.

- Evaluate usage honestly before the reminder date.

- Cancel if it's not essential or joyful.

- Keep a list of trials for future reference.

---

5. Use Public Libraries for Digital Content

Summary:
Access free eBooks, audiobooks, movies, and online courses through your local library system.

Why This Works:
Library apps like Libby and Hoopla offer thousands of free titles. This replaces or supplements paid reading, streaming, and learning subscriptions.

How to Do It:

- Get a free library card for each family member.

- Download apps like Libby, Hoopla, or Kanopy.

- Browse monthly as a family.

- Set "library night" once a week.

- Request books, movies, or courses to build engagement.

18. LEGAL & ADMINISTRATIVE COSTS

1. File Your Taxes Online for Free

Summary:
Use your country's certified or approved online platforms to file taxes at no cost—especially if your income and deductions are straightforward.

Why This Works:
For most middle-income families with standard employment or self-employment income, e-filing is fast, secure, and often free. Many governments or third-party partners offer digital tax tools to simplify the process and reduce errors.

How to Do It:

- Visit your government's official tax website to find a list of free or approved e-filing tools (e.g., IRS.gov in the U.S., HMRC.gov.uk in the U.K., ATO.gov.au in Australia).

- Register or log in to access pre-filled forms or tax return data if available.

- Follow the guided steps with built-in checks to minimize errors.

- File as early as possible to receive faster refunds and avoid last-minute stress.

- Save a digital or printed copy of your return for your records.

---

2. Use Legal Aid Clinics for Simple Matters

Summary:
Access free or low-cost legal advice for things like wills, tenants' rights, or notarization through community legal clinics.

Why This Works:
Legal clinics offer services for families at no cost, saving you hundreds on consultations or document prep.

How to Do It:

- Search online for legal aid clinics in your city or province.

- Call ahead to confirm eligibility and availability.

- Bring the necessary ID and documents.

- Prepare questions in advance.

- Follow up with any action steps they provide.

---

3. Write a Simple Will with a Template

Summary:
Use an online template or DIY kit to create a basic will that protects your family and assets.

Why This Works:
A lawyer-prepared will can cost $500–$1,000+. A clear, properly signed DIY will is legal in most provinces and a great starting point.

How to Do It:

- Choose a Canadian-specific will kit or service (like Willful or LegalWills.ca).

- List guardians, assets, and beneficiaries.

- Print and sign with two witnesses.

- Store safely and share with key family members.

- Update after significant life events.

---

4. Set Up Auto-Pay to Avoid Late Fees

Summary:
Automate recurring payments—especially for taxes, licenses, insurance, and utility bills—to avoid late fees, penalties, and service interruptions.

Why This Works:
Missing payment due to forgetfulness can result in fines ranging from minor fees to significant penalties, depending on the bill type. Automation ensures you're always on time, protecting your credit and saving money.

How to Do It:

- Log in to each service provider or your government's official payment portal.

- Enable auto-pay or set up email/SMS reminders for due dates.

- Link payments to a reliable, low-fee bank account or credit card.

- Review your payments monthly to catch errors or unexpected charges.

- Maintain a yearly checklist of all recurring obligations (e.g., taxes, vehicle registration, ID renewals).

---

5. Renew IDs and Passports Early

Summary:
Don't wait until the last minute to renew licenses, passports, or ID cards—rush fees add up fast.

Why This Works:
Expedited processing fees can double or triple standard rates. Early renewal avoids unnecessary costs and stress.

How to Do It:

- Mark expiry dates in your digital calendar.

- Set reminders 6 months in advance.

- Book appointments online when possible.

- Double-check required documents ahead of time.

- Use regular service unless travel is urgent.

19. PETS & ANIMAL CARE

1. Groom Your Pet at Home

Summary:
Skip the salon. Learn basic grooming skills to bathe, brush, and trim your pet yourself.

Why This Works:
Professional grooming can cost $50–$100 per visit. Home grooming saves hundreds yearly and strengthens your bond with your pet.

How to Do It:

- Buy a quality brush, pet shampoo, and nail clippers.

- Watch tutorials based on your pet's breed.

- Set up a consistent monthly routine.

- Use treats to make it positive.

- Practice patience—both of you are learning!

---

2. Buy Pet Food and Supplies in Bulk

Summary:
Stock up on your pet's essentials in bulk to save per unit and reduce last-minute store trips.

Why This Works:
Buying in larger quantities cuts the cost per serving. It also avoids emergency convenience store markups.

How to Do It:

- Compare prices at big box or online retailers.

- Store food in airtight containers for freshness.

- Rotate stock to avoid waste.

- Join loyalty or auto-ship programs for extra savings.

- Split bulk buys with a friend if storage is tight.

---

3. Prepare Homemade Treats and Meals

Summary:
Make simple dog or cat treats and meals at home using ingredients you already have.

Why This Works:
Homemade options can be healthier and cheaper—especially when using pantry staples or leftovers (with vet guidance).

How to Do It:

- Research safe ingredients (no onions, chocolate, grapes, etc.).

- Try easy recipes like pumpkin biscuits or rice with veggies.

- Freeze batches in portions.

- Avoid additives and keep it simple.

- Ask your vet about supplements if you are making full meals.

---

4. Create a Pet Health Fund

Summary:
Instead of relying only on pet insurance, set aside a small monthly amount for future vet visits or emergencies.

Why This Works:
Many pet owners aren't prepared for sudden $500–$2,000 vet bills. A personal fund gives flexibility and peace of mind.

How to Do It:

- Open a separate savings account or use a labelled envelope.

- Set up auto-transfers for $25–$50/month.

- Use it only for vet-related needs.

- Track expenses and adjust if needed.

- Keep vet estimates and receipts for future planning.

---

5. Compare Pet Insurance vs. Self-Insurance

Summary:
Evaluate whether monthly pet insurance premiums are worth it for your breed and budget—or if setting money aside is better.

Why This Works:
Pet insurance isn't right for every family. Some get better value by saving themselves and paying out of pocket.

How to Do It:

- Research multiple providers (e.g., Trupanion, Petsecure).

- Consider breed-specific risks and age.

- Compare premiums to vet costs likely.

- Weigh coverage caps and exclusions.

- Choose insurance only if it fits your risk tolerance.

20. TRAVEL & VACATION PLANNING

1. Use Credit Card Points Strategically

Summary:
Book flights, hotels, or rental cars using accumulated travel points from your credit card to offset vacation costs.

Why This Works:
Families can save hundreds—sometimes thousands—by leveraging rewards. Points often stretch further when redeemed for travel.

How to Do It:

- Choose a credit card with substantial travel rewards.

- Use it for regular expenses (and pay off monthly).

- Check point-to-dollar value before redeeming.

- Transfer points to airline/hotel partners when it boosts value.

- Set travel alerts for bonus point redemptions.

---

2. Travel During Off-Peak Times

Summary:
Avoid school breaks and holidays when booking flights or accommodations to get better deals and fewer crowds.

Why This Works:
Off-peak travel can save 30–60% compared to peak pricing. It also offers more flexibility in bookings and activities.

How to Do It:

- Plan trips for shoulder seasons (e.g., May or September).

- Leave mid-week instead of weekends.

- Set flexible travel dates when searching online.

- Use fare prediction tools to book ahead.

- Ask schools about homework flexibility for 1–2 missed days.

---

3. Book Accommodations with a Kitchenette

Summary:
Choose rentals or hotels with basic kitchen amenities so you can cook simple meals instead of dining out daily.

Why This Works:
Eating out as a family can cost $60–$100/day. Preparing breakfast, lunch, or snacks during your stay drastically cuts expenses.

How to Do It:

- Use Airbnb, Vrbo, or extended-stay hotels with a kitchen.

- Bring breakfast basics and reusable containers.

- Make a quick grocery stop when you arrive.

- Eat out once per day or only for special meals.

- Let kids "help cook" for fun.

---

4. Pack Snacks, Water, and Essentials

Summary:
Bring snacks, refillable water bottles, and travel items to avoid overpriced airport and convenience store purchases.

Why This Works:
Buying on-the-go snacks or small items can inflate your budget quickly. A $2 granola bar at home might be $8 in the airport.

How to Do It:

- Pack easy, TSA-friendly snacks in zip bags.

- Bring refillable water bottles for each family member.

- Include sunscreen, wipes, and over-the-counter meds.

- Use a packing list to avoid forgetting essentials.

- Designate a "snack captain" to manage food during the trip.

---

5. Try a Staycation or Nearby Getaway

Summary:
Enjoy a vacation vibe without leaving your city—book a local

hotel or explore parks, museums, and attractions close to home.

Why This Works:
You skip airfare and long travel days but still get quality time, adventure, and a mental reset at a fraction of the cost.

How to Do It:

- Book one or two nights at a local hotel with a pool.

- Plan themed days: nature hike, art day, food tour.

- Pack a suitcase to make it feel special.

- Involve the kids in itinerary planning.

- Set "no chores or errands" rules to keep it vacation-like.

21. TIME-SAVING SERVICES

1. Batch Cook Once, Eat Twice or More

Summary:
Dedicate time each week to cooking double portions so you can freeze or repurpose meals for later days.

Why This Works:
Batch cooking slashes meal prep time and reduces the temptation to order takeout—saving time and $20–$60 weekly.

How to Do It:

- Pick 2–3 freezer-friendly recipes per week.

- Cook double or triple quantities on Sundays.

- Portion into containers and label with dates.

- Reheat for lunch or dinner later in the week.

- Rotate meals to avoid repetition.

---

2. Replace Delivery Apps with Simple Meal Planning

Summary:
Plan a week's worth of meals and prep ingredients in advance to avoid costly food delivery "emergencies."

Why This Works:
Food delivery often costs 2–3x more than home cooking due to fees, tips, and markups. Planning removes the "what's for dinner?" stress.

How to Do It:

- Pick 4–5 easy meals everyone enjoys.

- Shop with a list to avoid midweek stops.

- Prep ingredients (like chopped veggies) ahead.

- Post your meal plan on the fridge.

- Keep 1-2 quick backup meals in the freezer.

---

3. Do a Weekly "Power Hour" of Errands

Summary:
 Batch your errands into one or two focused trips instead of scattering them throughout the week.

Why This Works:
Driving around daily wastes gas, time, and often leads to impulse purchases. One efficient trip per week keeps things simple and cheap.

How to Do It:

- Make a master errand list every Sunday.

- Group stops by location.

- Pick one low-traffic time slot (e.g., Wednesday evening).

- Bring snacks and water to stay on track.

- Involve kids as helpers or navigators.

---

4. Cancel Unused Convenience Subscriptions

Summary:
Pause or cancel meal kits, cleaning plans, laundry drop-offs, and any subscription that isn't used weekly.

Why This Works:
Many families forget about auto-renewed services. Even cancelling just one could instantly free up $30–$100/month.

How to Do It:

- Review credit card statements for recurring charges.

- Ask: "Are we using this every week?"

- Cancel directly in the app or email support.

- Set a calendar check-in each quarter to reassess.

- Replace with DIY or once-in-a-while alternatives.

---

5. Invest Once in Time-Saving Tools

Summary:
Buy quality tools—like a slow cooker, robot vacuum, or family calendar—that save time long-term without ongoing fees.

Why This Works:
One-time purchases often replace costly services. For example, a $75 slow cooker can eliminate weekly meal kits or restaurant orders.

How to Do It:

- List three time-heavy chores you'd love to simplify.

- Research affordable, durable tools for each.

- Read reviews and buy during sales.

- Learn how to use them with online videos.

- Track savings vs. former service costs.

22. MINDSET, HABITS & BEHAVIORAL FINANCE

1. Use a 30-day Wait List for Wants

Summary:
Before buying non-essentials, write them down and wait 30 days. If you still want the item later, consider it thoughtfully.

Why This Works:
Impulse buys often lose their appeal with time. This delay helps you identify emotional vs. intentional spending—and protects your budget.

How to Do It:

- Create a "wants" list in your notes app or notebook.

- Every time you're tempted, add it to the list instead.

- Revisit items after 30 days.

- Delete the ones you no longer care about.

- Only buy if it still fits your budget and values.

---

2. Run a No-Spend Weekend or Week

Summary:
Challenge yourself to spend nothing on non-essentials for a weekend or even a whole week—using what you already have.

Why This Works:
These "reset periods" reveal habits you don't realize that could cost you money and help reset your appreciation for what's enough.

How to Do It:

- Choose your no-spend dates and tell the family.

- Use pantry meals, DIY entertainment, and home routines.

- Avoid online shopping "browsing."

- Reflect on what was surprisingly easy.

- Celebrate the savings at the end!

---

3. Teach Kids to Budget with Their Allowance

Summary:
Break allowance into categories like save, spend, and share—teaching kids how to handle money with purpose and joy.

Why This Works:
Kids who learn budgeting early are more likely to become financially responsible adults. They learn that money is a tool—not a toy.

How to Do It:

- Give a weekly allowance with simple jars or envelopes.

- Help them label: "Saving," "Spending," and "Giving."

- Set savings goals together (e.g., a toy or book).

- Let them make small spending choices.

- Celebrate their milestones to reinforce habits.

---

4. Use Gratitude to Reduce Emotional Spending

Summary:
Practice gratitude journaling or daily reflection to focus on what you already have, reducing the desire for impulse purchases.

Why This Works:
Gratitude rewires the brain to focus on sufficiency. This lowers the urge to buy as a reaction to stress or boredom.

How to Do It:

- Write three things you're grateful for each evening.

- Share one with the family at dinner.

- Keep a "Joy List" of what brings happiness for free.

- Use gratitude as a tool before shopping online.

- Ask, "Do I need this—or am I just numbing something?"

---

5. Automate Good Habits, Not Just Bills

Summary:
Use automation to pay bills and build wealth—automatically transferring money into savings or investments.

Why This Works:
What's automatic becomes effortless. Families who automate savings remove the daily decision-making friction and grow wealth in the background.

How to Do It:

- Set up auto-transfer to a savings account on payday.

- Use a separate "don't touch" account for goals.

- Set up automatic monthly contributions to a tax-advantaged savings account (such as education or retirement plans available in your country).

- Start small—then increase over time.

- Review quarterly to celebrate progress.

23. NEEDS VS. WANTS (SMART SPENDING FRAMEWORK)

1. Know the Difference Between Needs and Wants

Summary:
One of the most effective lifelong money habits is learning to pause and ask: *"Is this a need or a want?"* This simple question creates clarity and control.

Why This Works:
Needs are essential—like food, shelter, health, or basic

transportation. Wants bring comfort or pleasure but often come with long-term costs. When families spend mindfully on needs and delay or downgrade wants, they create more room for savings, freedom, and peace of mind.

How to Do It:

- Before any purchase, ask: "Do we truly need this, or just want it?"

- Teach your kids to ask the same question—make it a family rule.

- Practice waiting 24 hours before buying wants.

- Revisit your monthly budget and highlight any wants you can pause, reduce, or replace.

- Use the savings toward your emergency fund, debt, or a meaningful goal.

www.ingramcontent.com/pod-product-compliance
Lightning Source LLC
Chambersburg PA
CBHW030532210326
41597CB00014B/1123